Survey of Urban Indicator Data 1970-1977

MICHAEL J. FLAX

823-1

February 1978

THE URBAN INSTITUTE
WASHINGTON, D.C.

The research and studies forming the basis for this paper were supported by the Ford Foundation.

The interpretations or conclusions are those of the author and should not be attributed to the Ford Foundation, or to The Urban Institute, its trustees, or other organizations that support its research.

ISBN 87766-214-2

UI 823-1

PLEASE REFER TO URI 21200 WHEN ORDERING

Available from:

Publications Office
The Urban Institute
2100 M Street, N.W.
Washington, D.C. 20037

List price: $3.50

COPYRIGHT © 1973
BY THE URBAN INSTITUTE

A/78/750

ABSTRACT

This report surveys two types of urban indicator reports: those devoted to the description of a single city or metropolitan area, and those that describe and compare several such jurisdictions. The reports are listed and categorized according to the type of organization issuing the report and the subject areas covered. There is also a short discussion of fiscal indicators that are used in rating various municipal bond offerings.

Since very few jurisdictions issue regular indicator reports, some of the factors that encourage or discourage such reports are discussed, and some possible alternatives are suggested.

ACKNOWLEDGMENTS

This report was written under the general direction of William Gorham, President of The Urban Institute. Further guidance was provided by Harold Guthrie, Harvey Garn, Michael Springer, and Henry Mortimer, all also of The Urban Institute.

Many of the documents were obtained from the libraries of the National League of Cities, the Center for the Coordination of Research on Social Indicators, and, of course, The Urban Institute. Some of the persons consulted in the Washington area were: Albert E. Gollin, Bureau of Social Science Research; A. Mindlin, Herbert Bixhorn, and Nathan Levy, all of the D.C. Government; Conrad Perlman, of the D.C. Planning Department; Leo Penne, Lawrence Williams, and James Glasser, of the National League of Cities; John Shannon, Advisory Committee on Intergovernmental Relations; Harold Goldsmith, National Institutes of Mental Health; William Rucker and David Sheatsley, Fairfax County Government; Nancy Carmichael, Center for Coordination of Research and Social Indicators; Harry Hatry and Harold King, The Urban Institute; and Daniel Tunstall, Consultant.

Others who provided documents or advice are associated with local governments and research institutions across the entire country. The list includes James Jamarillo, Jewell Jones, Skip Jones, Harry Schultz, Kenneth Ranney, Richard Conway, Larry Shadzinski, Patricia Becker, William Leetch, Glen Hartz, Jerry Blum, William Nevius, Ralph Webb, Nancy Mintner, Thomas Finney, Doris Zelinsky, Anthony Galiono, John Dedishaw, Richard Hanel, Donald Mazziato, Donald Colley, Ronald Frankum, Robert Ontell, Joseph Colley, and, generally, the Planning Departments of Tulsa, Oklahoma, and Redwood City, California.

I am indebted to Jacqueline Swingle for typing and scheduling numerous drafts and to the Institute Support Center for its prompt completion of the final document.

CONTENTS

Abstract	iii
Acknowledgments	v
1. Introduction	1
2. Intracity Indicator Reports	3
3. Intercity Comparison Indicator Reports	31
4. Fiscal Indicators	43
5. Other Intercity Reports	49
6. Discussion	51

EXHIBITS

1. Organizations Issuing Intracity Reports	19
2. Subject Areas by Different Classes of Organizations	20
3. Organizations Issuing Intercity Reports	32
4. Subject Areas by Different Classes of Organizations	33
5. Factors Used in Rating Municipal Bonds	45
6. The Meaning of Rating Symbols	46
7. Moody's Rating of Some Large Cities	47

1. INTRODUCTION

A cursory look at the field reveals that numerous urban indicator reports are prepared by a wide variety of local or national organizations, and that they appear very irregularly. This paper examines some of the characteristics of the indicator reports that have been generated over the past seven years, points out places where indicator work is being done, and comments on the possible uses and users of indicator data. Since very few cities publish regular indicator reports but many of them use indicator types of data, we will examine some factors that may explain this behavior.

As used in this paper, indicators are broad measures that are generally associated with outputs or outcomes and often include variables related to the concept of the "quality of life." They are primarily descriptive and are targeted for varied audiences ranging from "decision makers" to the general public. (Individual cities may produce such data under a variety of names.)

The following types of indicator reports will be described:

1. Intracity. The data are aggregated by geographic area (e.g., census tracts), client attributes (e.g., income, race, poverty), or different functions (police, health). Comparisons can be made over time or by different geographic or client attributes.

2. Intercity Comparisons. The data are disaggregated across cities or metropolitan areas. (For this paper we are limiting ourselves to reports that identify cities or metropolitan areas by name.) Comparisons can be made across cities or metropolitan areas, or cities can be compared with their suburbs. Reports can cover many subject areas or deal only with one.

3. _Fiscal Indicators_. These data deal with revenues, expenditures, and the debt and credit rating of cities. They may be focused on long-run trends, or on current fiscal conditions. There is disagreement as to the suitability of different municipal accounting procedures. We will describe some current problems and issues and also provide a list of commonly used fiscal indicators.

4. _Other Studies that Include Comparisons of Cities_. Some studies devoted to describing, explaining, or testing various political or sociological propositions include comparative data on cities. Thus, sometimes data on specified cities are included in reports on health, crime, or education. When data on specified cities are used in this manner it is often difficult to differentiate between "urban indicator" research and research in various fields or substantive areas.

This paper emphasizes the first category, intracity reports. First we present a bibliography of typical examples of this type of report, summarizing the subject areas chosen, the number of variables selected, and the analysis and presentation methods used. We then discuss some interesting studies and mention a few sources of data that might not be widely known.

We treat the intercity comparisons similarly, recognizing that there are differences from the previous category: a smaller number of reports exist; those who produce the intercity reports are not their primary users; and the data sources differ from the previous category.

In the case of fiscal indicators, we reference several key documents, present a listing of some common indicators, and describe some of the current substantive issues.

For the fourth category, other studies that include comparative urban data, we provide several typical examples.

2. INTRACITY INDICATOR REPORTS

The gathering of indicator documents led to problems in terminology. In practice we looked for documents that, regardless of their titles, described numerous aspects of a city. Thus, we included several "needs assessments" as well as "profiles" and "state of the city" reports. Some cities also conduct surveys which present citizens' views of city conditions (Columbus, Ohio, and in Michigan, Flint and Detroit).[1]

While gathering these documents, we were also looking for cities that issued regular (either yearly or biennial) reports. Such cities were unexpectedly hard to find, but six were finally located:[2] San Diego, Orange County, and Los Angeles in California; Flint, Michigan; Fairfax County, Virginia, and Montgomery County, Maryland.

Besides discussing some of the issues raised by these documents we list the 58 indicator reports we obtained and provide some summary data about them in the listing that follows. This data, while not very detailed, gives the reader some information about the document: the name of the city,[3] the agency producing the report, the subject areas covered, the number of variables used, the type of analysis used, how the data are presented, the number of pages, and the date produced.

While this list is not comprehensive, it does reflect a search through the pertinent literature in three libraries[4] and telephone calls to those cities that were believed to produce regular indicator reports.[5]

---

1. One source estimated that about 30 cities have had surveys done. Flint is the only city known to conduct such a survey regularly.

2. New Orleans is said to issue such a report every two years, but it has not been included since I have not been able to obtain a copy.

3. Many cities known to have active and competent planning departments do not issue profile or indicator reports. For instance, Dayton, Ohio, has many program-oriented documents but no "indicator" reports.

4. The Urban Institute, the National League of Cities, and the Center for Coordination of Research in Social Indicators.

5. See the Acknowledgments.

INTERCITY INDICATOR REPORTS

City Reporting	Subject Areas	Number of Variables of Tables	Analysis Used	Presentation	Comments
1. ALBUQUERQUE, NEW MEXICO. McNamara, Patrick, A Social Report for Metropolitan Albuquerque, The Albuquerque Urban Observatory, January 1973, 114 pp.	Employment and the Economy; Criminal Justice; Housing; Health; Air Pollution; Education. (6)	231 tabs.	Data are analyzed differently for each area. Some health data are reviewed over the past ten years.	A wide array of tables and graphs	No cohesiveness to this report, although it contains interesting data.
2. ALLENTOWN, PA. Development of Neighborhood Indicators, Allentown Urban Observatory, January 1976, 103 pp.	Housing. (1)	35 tabs.	Compared citizen survey with a Delphi of officials.* Also used city's housing data bank.	Maps and tables	Good synthesis of theory and practical needs of city.
3. ATLANTA, GEORGIA. Census Use Study: Social and Health Indicators System, Atlanta: Part 2, Office of Economic Opportunity and the Bureau of the Census, October 1973, 209 pp.	Health; Welfare; Education; Transportation; Taxation; Crime. (6)	40 tabs.	Comparisons are made between primary area (4 census tracts with poverty programs) and comparison area (7 tracts, similar, but with no poverty programs).	Graphs and tabulations	Special programs were used to allocate data to small areas.
4. AUSTIN, TEX. Lorna Monti, Social Indicators for Austin, Texas: A Cluster Analysis of Census Tracts, Bureau of Business Research, Graduate School of Business, The University of Texas at Austin, 1975, 49 pp.	Demography; Income; Education; Change Pattern; Housing; Health; Safety. (7)	38 vars.	Computer selection of clusters of census tracts.	Maps and tables	Good use of computers to develop easily understood presentation.
5. COLORADO SPRINGS, COLO. Special Environment Audit of Colorado Springs, Colorado College Student Group, Summer 1975, 185 pp.	Physical, Political, and Demographic Environments; Citizen Perceptions. (4)	23 categories. Used wide variety of data from varied services.	Used a citizen survey.	Maps, graphs, and tables	Good coverage but fragmented since each selection was written by a different student.

* That is, using laymen as a jury and experts as witnesses.

INTERCITY INDICATOR REPORTS

City Reporting	Subject Areas	Number of Variables or Tables	Analysis Used	Presentation	Comments
6. COLUMBUS, OHIO. Benchmark: Aspects of the Quality of Life in Metropolitan Columbus, 1973, 179 pp.	Education; Health; Employment; Income; Transportation; Crime; Diversity; Housing; Police. (9)	122 tabs.	Based on a comprehensive sample survey.	Graphs and tables (very thorough)	Use of many survey techniques. Thorough for each area.
7. DENVER, COLO. Urban Social Indicators: Selected Conditions and Trends in Denver and Its Metropolitan Area, Denver Urban Observatory, June 1973, 67 pp.	Physical Environment; Health; Public Safety; Education; Housing; Employment and Income. (6)	42 tabs.	Comparisons with other cities and overtime.	Tables	Good discussion of the derivation of indicators.
8. DENVER, COLO. Social Indicators, First Year Report on Housing and Employment in Denver and the Denver Metropolitan Area, Denver Urban Observatory, May 1972, 40 pp.	Housing; Employment. (2)	20 vars.	A detailed discussion of what was done.	Tables	Used only decennial census data.
9. DETROIT, MICH. Detroit Housing Needs As Seen By The Urban Collective, New Detroit Incorporated, August 1973. 87 pp.	Housing; Demography. (2)	31 tabs.	Choice of indicators stems from discussion of how the housing market operates. Also forecasts for 1981.	Tables and graphs	Good discussion of possible causal mechanisms.
10. DETROIT, MICH. Michigan Health Survey: Detroit (March 1970-May 1972), Center for Health Statistics, Mich. Dept. of Public Health, Detroit City Health Dept., 1973, 42 pp.	Demography; Health. (2)	34 tabs.	Sample survey.	Tables	This survey was formerly known as the ECHO survey (Evidence for Community Health Organization).

INTRACITY INDICATOR REPORTS

City Reporting	Subject Areas	Number of Variables or Tables	Analysis Used	Presentation	Comments
11. DETROIT, MICH. Michigan Health Survey, Detroit 1972, 1973, 25 pp.	Demography; Household Information; Health. (3)	28 tabs.	Sample survey.	Tables	A presentation of results of the ECHO survey (Evidence for Community Health Organization).
12. DURHAM, N.C. Durham Urban Observatory Report: Analysis of Crime Incidence in Relationship to Selective Public Services and Demographic Characteristics in Durham, North Carolina. N.C. Central University, Durham, N.C., June 1976, 36 pp.	The determinants of crime. (1)	14 vars.	Stepwise multiple regression with various crimes as the dependent variable.	Maps and tables	Found that education and density per acre were best predictors of a combination of various crimes.
13. FAIRFAX COUNTY, VA. David W. Sheatsley, Fairfax County Profile, Community Development Branch, Office of Research and Statistics, 1977, 130 pp.	Population; Education; Employment; Income; Revenues; Expenditures; Housing. (7)	114 tabs.	Comparisons with jurisdictions.	Tables	Compares Fairfax with Virginia and Washington SMSA jurisdictions.
14. FLINT, MICH. Human Well-Being in Flint, 1973, Evidence for Community Health Organization (ECHO Survey), 1974, 32 pp.	Housing; Population; Income; Unemployment; Employment; Health. (6)	25 vars.	Comparisons by areas in the city.	Uses computer generated maps	Separate maps for each variable. Hard to see the effects of many variables on a single city area.

- 7 -

INTERCITY INDICATOR REPORTS

City Reporting	Subject Area	Number of Variables or Tables	Analysis Used	Presentation	Comments
15. FRESNO, CALIF. Community Profile 1973, Management Systems Office, City of Fresno, 1974, 53 pp.	Demography; Health; Education; Social Behavior; Income; Employment; Economy; Government; Transportation; Construction; Finance. (11)	70 tabs.	Text related to data presented.	Maps, graphs, and tables	Good use of a wide variety of data and presentation techniques.
16. FRESNO-CLOVIS, CALIF. 1973 Citizen Survey: Problem Ranking/Rating, Fresno Community Analysis Division, 1974, 24 pp.	Income; Jobs; Environmental Quality; Housing; Police Relations; Health Care. (6)	83 questions	Sample survey disaggregated to five neighborhood areas.	Maps and tables	Good presentation of information about different areas of the city.
17. GAINESVILLE, FLA. Dickenson, Gray, and Smith, "The Quality of Life in Gainesville, Florida: An Application of Territorial Social Indicators," Southern Geographer, vol. 12, no. 2, pp. 121-132.	Housing; Family; Crime; Health; Poverty. (5)	17 vars.	For each subject area a composite index was developed for each census enumeration district. One summary indicator of the quality of life was also developed for each district.	Maps	
18. GARDEN GROVE, CALIF. Appendix to the Community Needs Assessment Study (Partial Preliminary Draft), Human Resources Commission, July 1976, 77 pp.	Demography; Income; Employment; Housing; Pollution; Transportation; Redevelopment. (7)	77 tabs.	Descriptive statistics presented.	Tables and graphs	No text.

INTRACITY INDICATOR REPORTS

City Reporting	Subject Areas	Number of Variables or Tables	Analysis Used	Presentation	Comments
19. KANSAS CITY, MO. A Social Report for Central Portions of Kansas City Area: Testing and Reporting of Governmental Indices, Mid-America Urban Observatory, 1973, 359 pp.	Housing; Pollution; Physical Health; Mental Health; Education; Economy; Welfare; Family Conflict; Public Safety; Quality of Life Index. (10)	200 vars.	Text for each area. Factor analysis for quality of life.	Tables (hard to integrate with the text)	Presentation of the relationship between policy recommendations and indicators is weak.
20. LOS ANGELES, CALIF. The State of the City: A Cluster Analysis of Los Angeles, A Report by the Los Angeles Community Analysis Bureau, June 1974, 180 pp.	Identified and named neighborhoods (e.g., post-war suburbs, the suburbanites, high income; subsidized housing; etc. (30)	66 vars.	Computer cluster analysis of similar census tracts.	Maps and tables	Complex mathematics is presented so it is easily understood.
21. LOS ANGELES, CALIF. An Analysis of the Blighted Communities of Los Angeles, Community Analysis Bureau, City of Los Angeles, Feb. 1973, 50 pp.	4 clusters related to poverty.	40 vars.	Used scores on ambience, stress, alienation, and poverty to identify blighted communities.	Maps and tables	Text on 26 blighted communities.
22. MECKLENBURG COUNTY, N.C. Moroney, Maloney, and May, Social Planning Use of Urban Planning Information Systems: Phase I. Analysis of Social Need in Mecklenburg County, Sept. 1972, 63 pp.	Socio-economic Status variable (SES) derived.	5 vars.	Census tracts are classified as to their SES quality.	Maps and tables	

- 8 -

INTERCITY INDICATOR REPORTS

City Reporting	Subject Areas	Number of Variables or Tables	Analysis Used	Presentation	Comments
23. MILWAUKEE, WISC. Selected Socioeconomic Indicators of Milwaukee County, Wisconsin: A Comparative Report, University of Wisconsin Extension, Summer 1973, 100 pp.	Population Stability; Age; Race; Occupation; Labor Force; Crime; Education; Housing; Families; Fertility; Mortality. (11)	71 vars.	71 Variables ranked for 43 neighborhoods or community areas in the Milwaukee SMSA.	Tables	Straightforward presentation.
24. MILWAUKEE, WISC. A Social Report for Milwaukee: Trends and Indicators, Milwaukee Urban Observatory, 1973-1974, 107 pp.	Population; Housing; Economics, Education; Health; Public Safety. (6)	41 vars.	Comparisons over time and between different demographic groups.	Graphs, tables, and maps	
25. MILWAUKEE, WISC. Karl Flaming, Toward A Social Report for Milwaukee, Milwaukee Urban Observatory, Summer 1972, 118 pp.	Housing. (1)	No data	Discusses indicators and their possible uses.	Graphs illustrate theory	
26. MINNEAPOLIS, MINN. 1973 Annual Report, First National Bank of Minneapolis, 1974, 24 pp.	Jobs; Income; Health; Public Safety; Housing; Education; Participation; Environment; Transportation; Culture; Human Relations; Community Commitment; Consumer Protection. (13)	60 vars.	Deals only with areas the bank can influence. Sets objectives for next year.	Compact two-page chart	Well thought out and relevant.

INTERCITY INDICATOR REPORTS

City Reporting	Subject Areas	Number of Variables or Tables	Analysis Used	Presentation	Comments
27. MINNEAPOLIS, MINN. 1972 Annual Report, First National Bank of Minneapolis, 1973, 24 pp.	Jobs; Income; Health; Public Safety; Housing; Education; Participation; Environment; Transportation. (9)	28 vars.	Data for St. Paul, Minneapolis and their suburbs are presented and compared.	Compact two-page chart	Good condensation of numerous indicators.
28. MONTGOMERY COUNTY, MD. 1977 Statistical Profile, Chief Administrative Office, Management and Public Policy, July 1977, 197 pp.	Population; Employment; Agriculture; Manufacturing; Retail Sales; Income; Housing; Public Finance; Education; Public Safety; Health; Transportation; Environment; Recreation; Energy. (15)	151 tabs.	Comparisons and breakdowns.	Tables and maps	A wide variety of statistics. This report is issued yearly.
29. NASHVILLE, TENN. How Well Is Metro Doing? Metropolitan Government of Nashville-Davidson County, 1976, 55 pp.	Policy Protection; Fire Protection; Water and Wastewater; Refuse Collection; Transportation; Libraries; Recreation. (7)	46 vars.	Compared over three years. Expanded version of the 1975 report listed below.	Used maps as well as graphs	Measures more meaningful since compared over time.

INTERCITY INDICATOR REPORTS

City Reporting	Subject Areas	Number of Variables or Tables	Analysis Used	Presentation	Comments
30. NASHVILLE, TENN. *How Well Is Metro Doing?* Department of Finance, Metropolitan Government of Nashville-Davidson County, 1975, 40 pp.	Police Protection; Fire Protection; Water and Wastewater; Refuse Collection; Transportation; Recreation; Libraries. (7)	54 vars.	Focused on activities city could influence. Surveys were used for some measures.	Graphs	Much thought went into the design of the performance measures used.
31. NASHVILLE, TENN. Hermanson et al. *State of a Metropolitan Government: Urban Indicators and Social Change*, The Urban Observatory of Metropolitan Nashville-University Centers, Dec. 1973, 337 pp.	Household; Education; Air Pollution; Health; Public Safety; Housing; Labor. (7)	106 tabs.	Tabulations and ranking. Used citizen survey.	Tables and graphs	Comprehensive and clear narrative.
32. NEW YORK CITY. *The Quality of Life in Urban America; New York City: A Regional and National Comparative Analysis*, The City of New York, Office of the Mayor, Office of Administration, May 1971, vol. 1, 92 pp.	Crime; Environment; Revenue; Taxation; Social Services. (5)	60 tabs.	New York compared with other cities (often seems biased toward New York).	Tables and graphs (ranking)	Interesting data from a wide variety of sources.
33. NEW YORK CITY. *The Quality of Life in Urban America; New York City: A Regional and National Comparative Analysis*, City of New York, Office of the Mayor, Office of Administration, 1971, vol. 2, 36 pp.	Demand for Office Space in Manhattan; Lead Poisoning; Electric Power; Transportation; Medical Care; Work Stoppages. (6)	40 tabs.	Comparisons of New York City with other cities (often seems biased toward New York).	Tables and graphs (ranking)	Interesting data from a wide variety of sources.

INTRACITY INDICATOR REPORTS

City Reporting	Subject Areas	Number of Variables or Tables	Analysis Used	Presentation	Comments
34. NEW YORK CITY. Community Planning District Profiles: Part I - Population and Housing, New York City Planning Commission, April 1973, 50 pp.	Population; Housing. (2)	40 vars.	Data is presented for 62 Community Planning Districts (CPD's).	Tables with maps of CPD's	Uses census data.
35. NEW YORK CITY. Community Planning District Profiles, Part II: Socioeconomic Characteristics, New York City Planning Commission, May 1973, 50 pp.	Education; Income; Occupations; Labor Force Participation. (4)	29 vars.	Data is presented for 62 Community Planning Districts (CPD's).	Tables with maps of CPD's	Similar to Part I.
36. ORANGE COUNTY, CALIF. 1976-77 Report on the State of the County, vol. 6, Orange County Board of Supervisors, Jan. 1977, 174 pp.	Youth; Economy; Social and Demographic; Senior Citizens. (4)	137 tabs., graphs, and maps	Tables and text. Uses cluster analysis for many maps.	Tables, graphs, and maps	A wide assortment of presentation techniques. This report is issued yearly.
37. ORANGE COUNTY, CALIF. Report on The State of the County, 1976, vol. 5, Orange County Board of Supervisors, 1976, 185 pp.	Infant and Child Health; Substance Abuse; Youth; Senior Citizens; Veterans; the Disabled. (6)	179 tabs. and maps	Uses maps with overlays. Good text.	Maps, tables, and graphs	In actuality a sophisticated needs analysis study. Similar to report listed above.
38. ORANGE COUNTY, CALIF. 1976 Orange County Progress Report, vol. 13, June 1976, 82 pp.	Government; Population; Human Services; Construction; Economics. (5)	60 tabs. and other displays	Description and references.	Tables, charts, graphs, and maps	References as well as indicator data. This report is issued yearly.

- 13 -

INTRACITY INDICATOR REPORTS

City Reporting	Subject Areas	Number of Variables or Tables	Analysis Used	Presentation	Comments
39. ORANGE COUNTY, CALIF. 1975 Orange County Progress Report, vol. 12, Board of Supervisors, Orange County, Oct. 1975, 80 pp.	Government; Population; Human Services; Construction; Economy. (5)	60 tabs. and other displays	Descriptive.	Tables, charts, graphs, and maps	Much reference material (e.g., voter registration information) as well as more usual indicator data. Similar to report listed above.
40. PHILADELPHIA, PA. Gudaitis and Spaeth, A Socioeconomic Analysis of Fifteen Philadelphia Neighborhoods, Greater Philadelphia Federation of Settlements, 1976, 21 pp.	Economic; Population; Racial Concentration; Transiency; Youth Population; Family Orientation; Community Instability; Occupation. (8)	34 vars.	Used factor analysis to produce composite score for each neighborhood.	Used tables to show how each of 15 neighborhoods compared with other areas and the entire city	Only census data used, but local leaders queried on data preferences.
41. PROVIDENCE, R.I. Social Change Index Study Project, Rhode Island Council of Community Services, June 1974, 150 pp.	Developing an index of social change	6 vars.	Takes the geometric mean of 6 indicators of social stress.	Tables	Not particularly convincing.
42. SAN DIEGO, CALIF. Toward a Social Report on Young Children, Urban Observatory Press, March 1977, 134 pp.	Family Resources; Supplementary Child Care; Health; Learning; Mental Health. (5)	43 tabs.	Text with illustrative tables.	Tables	
43. SAN DIEGO, CALIF. The Quality of Life of the Elderly in San Diego County, The Urban Observatory Press, March 1977, 99 pp.	Demography; Income; Health; Housing; Transportation; Crime. (6)	26 tabs.	Text with illustrative data.	Tables	

INTRACITY INDICATOR REPORTS

City Reporting	Subject Areas	Number of Variables or Tables	Analysis Used	Presentation	Comments
44. SAN DIEGO, CALIF. Status of Women, Quality of Life in San Diego, 1976, Urban Observatory Press, Nov. 1976 290 pp.	Population; Education; Employment; Physical Health; Mental Health; Crime; Social Disorganization.	57 tabs.	Text with illustrative figures.	Tables	Advocacy in tone.
45. SAN DIEGO, CALIF. Quality of Life in San Diego - 1975, Status of Women: Selected Indicators and Trends, Urban Observatory Press, Oct. 1975, 47 pp.	Employment; Education; Births; Abortions; Social Disorganization. (5)	14 vars.	Mostly discussion. Little data.	Tables and charts	
46. SAN DIEGO, CALIF. The Quality of Life in San Diego: Selected Indicators of Urban Conditions and Trends 1973, The Urban Observatory of San Diego, March 1973, 336 pp.	Health; Education; Public Order; Housing; Physical Environment. (5)	122 tabs.	A wide variety of cross tabulations and comparisons.	Tables and graphs	Thorough job.
47. SAN DIEGO, CALIF. Toward a Social Report For The City of San Diego, The Urban Observatory of San Diego, 1972, 187 pp.	Health; Education; Welfare; Public Order; Housing; Physical Environment. (6)	16 tabs.	Text and tabular presentation of data variations over time.	Tables	Little data.
48. STOCKTON, CALIF. Profile Number 1, Crime in Stockton, vol. 1, City Planning, Stockton, Calif., July 1972 (vol. 1, 45 pp.; vol. 2, 139 pp.)	19 different types of crimes	Summary tables, maps showing distribution of each type of crime throughout the city.	Crime by city area.	Mostly maps	Thorough job. Vol 2 disaggregates down to a census tract level.

INTERCITY INDICATOR REPORTS

City Reporting	Subject Areas	Number of Variables or Tables	Analysis Used	Presentation	Comments
49. STOCKTON, CALIF. Neighborhood Analysis Program, Profile Number 2, Abstract Housing Dispersement Study, City of Stockton, 1973, 17 pp.	Housing. (1)	10 vars.	A discussion of housing causes and effects.	Charts, graphs, and maps	Contains projections in addition to current data.
50. STOCKTON, CALIF. Profile 3, Public Assistance, City of Stockton Neighborhood Analysis Program, 1974, 73 pp.	Public Assistance. (1)	24 tabs.	This study looks at the welfare load in California counties, discusses the causes, and projects future loads for Stockton.	Tables, maps, and graphs	Emphasizes discussion of factors leading to dependency.
51. STOCKTON, CALIF. Education Study, Profile Number 2, City of Stockton Neighborhood Analysis Program, March 1974, 126 pp.	Education: enrollment, dropouts, and attainment. (1)	44 tabs.	Describes education recipients and the education industry.	Maps and tables	Estimates future changes in enrollment.
52. TAMPA FLA. D. Smith and R. Gray, Social Indicators for Tampa, Florida, Urban Studies Bureau, University of Florida, May 1972, 80 pp.	Economic Status; Environment; Health; Education; Social Disorganization; Participation. (6)	47 vars.	Factor analysis to 4 factors.	Maps and tables	
53. TOKYO, JAPAN. Naoki Komuro, A Social Indicator of The Tokyo Metropolitan Area--An Attempt to Construct a One Dimensional Welfare Indicator, Japan Economic Research Institute, 1974, 12 pp.	Health; Income; Labor; Leisure; Public Order; and more not specified.	No specific variables are defined in this theoretical report.	Uses "Jury Delphi." Graphical method of weighting to develop one composite welfare indicator.	Graphs	A "Jury Delphi" uses laymen as jury, and experts as witnesses.

INTRACITY INDICATOR REPORTS

City Reporting	Subject Areas	Number of Variables or Tables	Analysis Used	Presentation	Comments
54. TOLEDO, OHIO. *Toledo Public Opinion Survey, 1976*, Toledo Management Services, June 1977, 13 pp. mimeographed.	Social; Health; Recreation; Garbage Collection; Police; Housing; Taxes; Participation in Sport. (8)	60 ques.	Descriptive only. Cross-tabulations planned but not done.	Tables	Straightforward presentation of the survey results.
55. WASHINGTON METROPOLITAN AREA. Gollin and Dixon, *Social Patterns and Attitudes in Greater Washington, 1973/1975: A Social Indicator Sourcebook*, The Washington Survey, Bureau of Social Science Research, Inc. Washington, D.C., 1975, 175 pp.	Demography; Personal; Transportation; Public Services; Police; Participation; The Media; Social Issues. (8)	31 vars.	Results arranged according to different area jurisdictions. 1973 and 1975 sample survey data are presented separately.	Tables (data appeared in the *Washington Post*)	Good presentation.
56. WASHINGTON, D.C. *A Social Indicator System for the District of Columbia: A Pilot Project*, District of Columbia Executive Office; Office of Planning and Management, Statistical Systems Group, April 1973, 115 pp.	Health; Housing; Socioeconomic Conditions; Dependence. (4)	17 vars.	Several variables are statistically sorted into four composite indicators.	Maps, charts, and tables	Clusters overlaid on a map of the area. Analysis is by composite indicators and by specified geographical area.
57. WASHINGTON, D.C. *The State of Human Resources in the District of Columbia*, A Report to the D.C. Department of Human Resources by the Washington Center for Metropolitan Studies, June 1971, 242 pp.	Population; Needs of Youth; Health Programs (3)	31 tabs.	Discussion in terms of needs and programs	Text and tables	Report targeted toward needs and resources of Department of Human Resources.

INTRACITY INDICATOR REPORTS

City Reporting	Subject Areas	Number of Variables or Tables	Analysis Used	Presentation	Comments
58. WICHITA, KANS. Wichita Profile 1970, Wichita Metropolitan Information Bulletin, no. 2, Oct. 1972, 33 pp.	Demography; Race; Socioeconomic Status; Housing; Unemployment; Occupation. (6)	52 maps and graphs	Use of census data related to text.	Multicolored maps and graphs	There are other "Chamber of Commerce" types of documents available that give further data on Wichita.

Observing exhibit 1, note that we can logically simplify our analysis by dividing our reports into the "academically oriented" (a university research center or a university-based urban observatory) and the "municipally oriented" (a city department or planning agency).[6] We observe that there are almost the same number of each--25 and 27. In exhibit 2 the subject areas covered by reports from these academic and municipal sources are compared. Again there are few differences. This may be due to the general availability of certain well-known data series. Some of the differences that do occur may stem from the fact that perceptions of causality vary with the perceiver's experience or training. Authors, moreover, vary in creativity and persistence.

After the variables have been decided on, there is the question of how or whether they should be combined. The use of individual measures has the advantage of clarity, because the reader knows what is being measured. Alternatively, measures can be combined on an equal or weighted basis to permit a single variable to encompass several aspects of a given subject area, although what is actually being encompassed is not always clear. Further, the measures can be converted to "Z" scores which enables their variation from the mean to be compared with other measurements. Finally, one can use factor analysis or cluster analysis to establish dimensions or to group similar characteristics. The resulting data can then be presented in the form of tables (ranked or not), in the form of graphs, or as maps.

The use of maps is an interesting device. For example, the Flint report (see no. 14, above) presents a series of twenty-three variables, each on a computer-generated map where the darkness of different map areas represents

---

6. In this breakdown, we do not include the "other" category since these organizations showed large but nonsystematic variations.

Exhibit 1

ORGANIZATIONS ISSUING
INTRACITY REPORTS

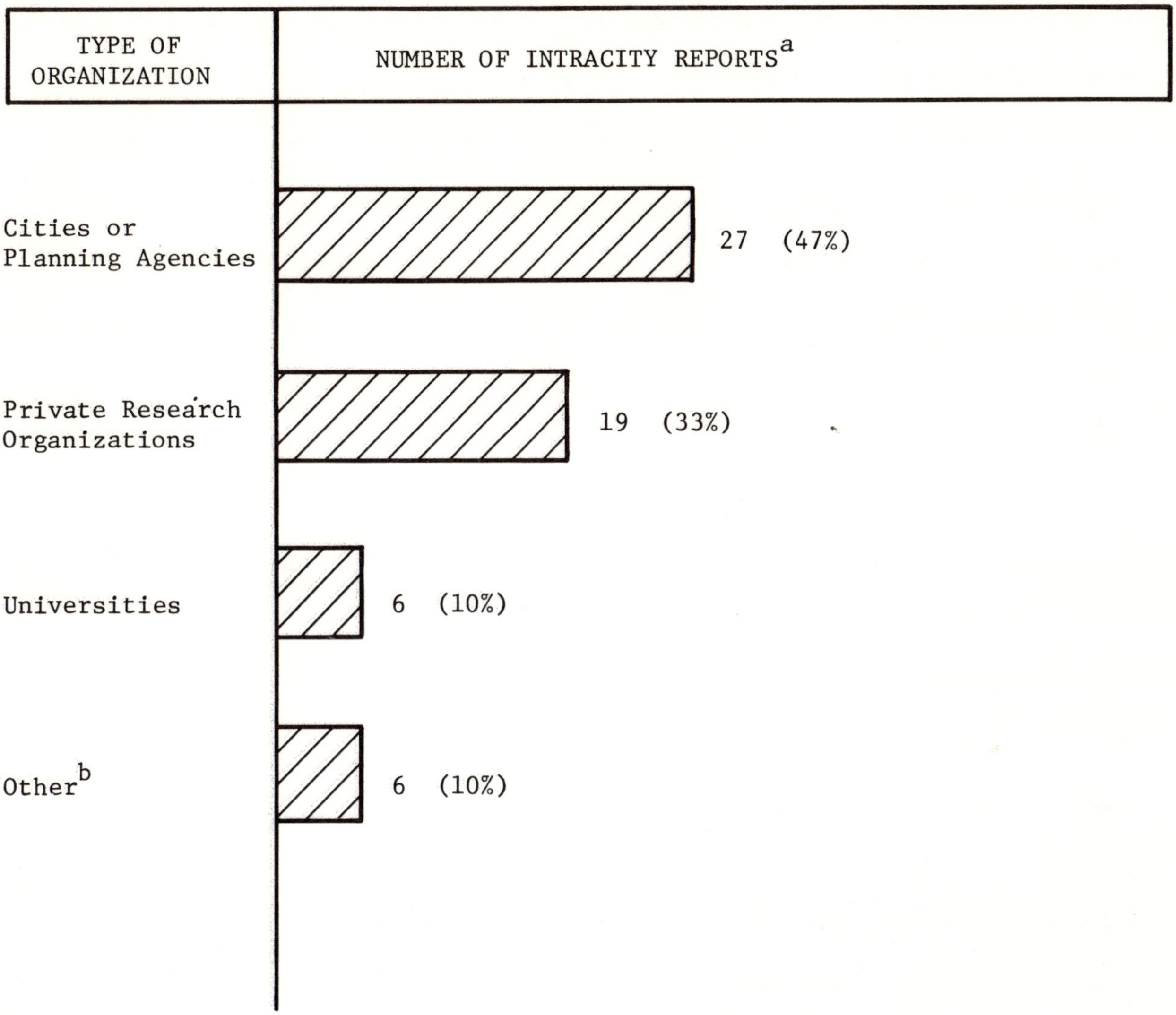

TYPE OF ORGANIZATION	NUMBER OF INTRACITY REPORTS[a]
Cities or Planning Agencies	27 (47%)
Private Research Organizations	19 (33%)
Universities	6 (10%)
Other[b]	6 (10%)

a. Out of a total of 58.
b. Includes charitable organizations, banks, etc.

Exhibit 2

SUBJECT AREAS BY
DIFFERENT CLASSES OF ORGANIZATIONS

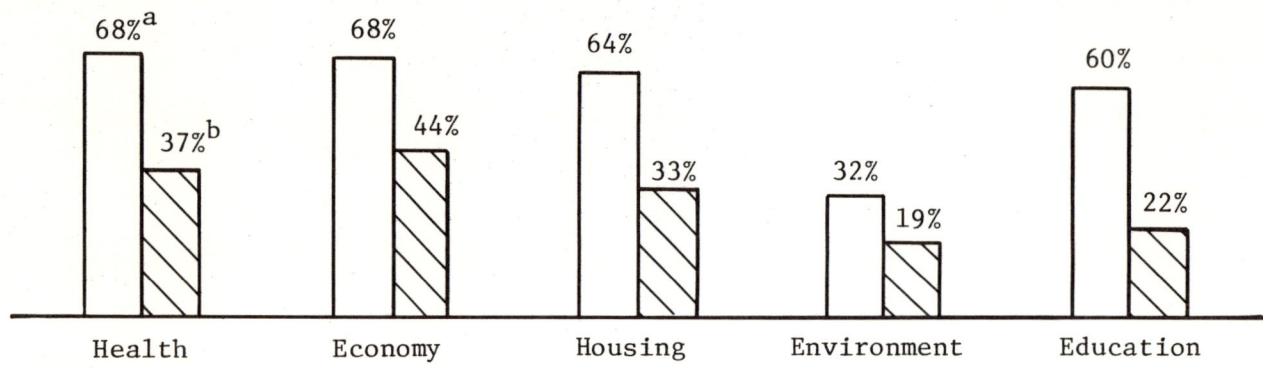

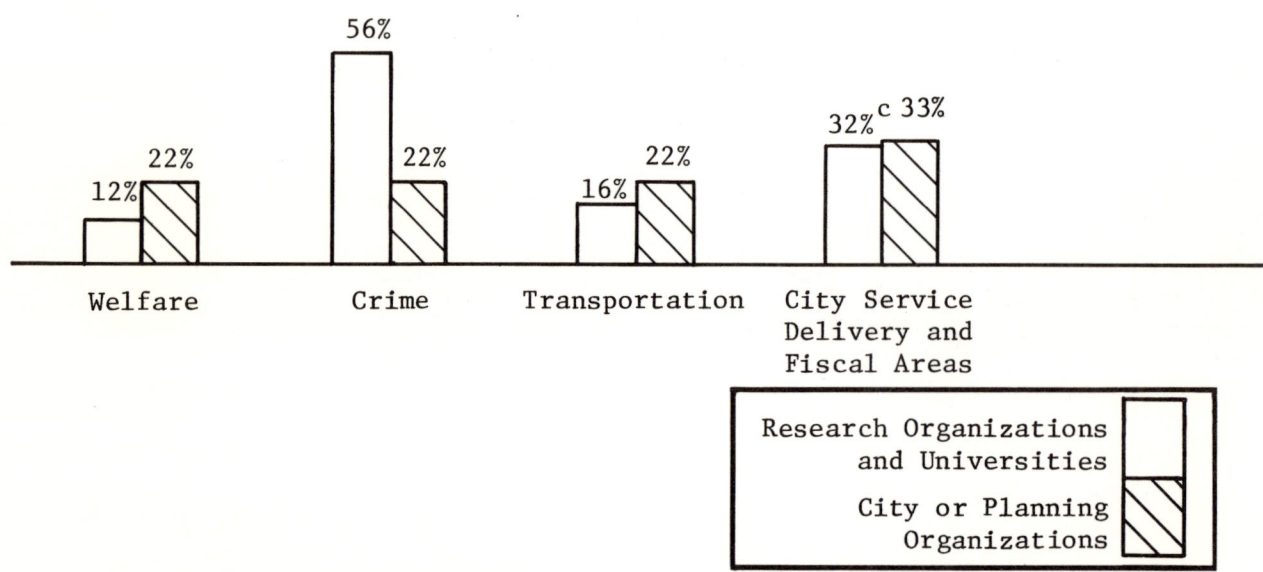

a. Of the 25 reports, 68 percent dealt with the health area.
b. Of the 29 reports, 37 percent dealt with the health area.
c. Of the 25 reports, 32 percent, while dealing with some of the subjects covered by this exhibit, also dealt with areas not covered here.

different magnitudes of the variable in different areas of the city. However, this type of presentation makes it difficult for the reader to see how any one area in the city is affected by all or many of the variables.

A report for the District of Columbia (see no. 56) alleviates this difficulty by using composite indicators for socioeconomic conditions and degrees of dependency and plotting them on maps, but by also providing summary tabulations for each census tract, so the reader can look at either the citywide variation of an indicator or at the levels of several indicators in a single census tract.

Two other reports illustrate the principle of clustering variables and presenting them on a map. The Austin, Texas, report (see no. 4) first selects certain measures (four housing measures,[7] for example, and then tests every census tract and selects those most similar on these four variables. The resulting clusters of census tracts are darkened in on a map of the city. Clusters such as this are derived for demographic, income, education, change pattern, health and safety factors and are similarly plotted on maps. This methodology provides a sense of the location of unfavorable and favorable conditions in the city.

A similar methodology, but on a larger scale, is used in Los Angeles (report no. 20). Thirty different clusters representing a wide variety of conditions (such as concentrations of subsidized housing, of single adults of Los Angeles, or Chinese people) are portrayed on maps and then summarized in tables.

Several other of the intracity reports use an innovative display technology. One is the Fresno report (see no. 15) in which mapping is used to

---

7. Median rent, median value of house, per capita needed improvements, and median age in years.

show variations in conditions in different geographical areas, and graphs and charts to show magnitudes and changes in the data.

It is interesting to note that Orange County, California (one of the six jurisdictions mentioned earlier as issuing regular indicator reports) issues two yearly indicator reports, both in well designed presentation formats. One (see no. 37) provides data about veterans, the disabled, senior citizens, etc, for a needs study. This report comes with two plastic overlays (census tracts and planning district) that can be placed over its maps. The other (no. 38) provides data on government, population, human services, construction, and economics. It uses tables and graphs in the presentation of data.

Clear and comprehensive reports were produced by Stockton, Calif., on crime, housing, public assistance, and education (see nos. 48-51). A non-theoretical, but thorough, treatment of housing was produced by Detroit, Mich. (see no. 9), and by Allentown, Pa. (see no. 2). Also, the Columbus report (no. 6) presents the results of a citizen survey in a clear and usable format. Two especially thorough reports were issued by Nashville (no. 31), and by San Diego (no. 46).

Another type of report deserves further mention. Issued for two consecutive years by the City of Nashville (although now discontinued), it seemed to move toward an evaluative function, rather than being primarily descriptive as in the other reports so far described. This report deals with those aspects of the quality of life that are under the control of the local government and attempts to evaluate the performance of the local government. For example, in the Nashville Annual Reports, How Well Is Metro Doing? (nos. 29 and 30), crime, fire control, water and wastewater, transportation (mostly auto), recreation, and libraries are covered. The measures used attempt to give some indication of how well the metropolitan government is doing its job.

Thus, they include citizen satisfaction with police and parks, figures on unreported crime, and arrests that do not lead to conviction. These reports are unusual in the manner in which the areas covered are chosen and in the measures used.

Although not included in our list of intracity indicator reports, there are similar types of reports that appear in local newspapers. On December 2, 1974, the New York Times printed a series of articles which included maps giving the location and rates of various crimes throughout New York City. Similar stories and maps covering health conditions and the allocation of city funds or personnel were also published.

Most recently on August 27, 1977 the Times published the fourth in a series of articles based on the Times/CBS poll of 2,171 New Yorkers. In this case they dealt with citizen reactions to the looting during the July blackout. These responses were related to the candidates the respondent favored in the upcoming mayoralty primary.

On the next day the Times published a front page report based on a New York police study of the characteristics of murder victims. The story included a map showing the number of homicides in each police precinct.

The Washington Post in conjunction with the Center for Metropolitan Studies has also run a series of articles based on a poll of residents throughout the Washington Metropolitan Area, and has presented comparative data for different jurisdictions.[8] Also in recent years the Washington Star has published a "Guide to Washington" based on a series of articles that

---

8. Some of the other newspapers running polls are the Minneapolis Tribune (the Minnesota Poll), the New York Daily News (Political Poll), Chicago Sun Times (Political Poll), and the Los Angeles Times and the San Francisco Chronical (the Field Poll).

appeared in the paper. The articles have covered topics such as shopping, traffic, and the characteristics of different areas of the city and the suburbs. The possibility of using newspapers as a means of transmitting indicator information to the public will be discussed later in this report.

Another alternative to regularly publishing indicator reports has been adopted by Inglewood, California. The city has established a management information center in which updated charts and maps are displayed. It is used by staff as well as citizens. When a particular issue is being discussed or disputed the parties involved are invited to use the information available at the center.[9]

There are several available sources supplying data that might be usefully incorporated in a city's social indicator report or used to supplement it. Although some of the data are based on the decennial census and so are sometimes out of date and unsuited to measure short term changes, the content may broaden the type of analysis conducted.[10]

A National Institute of Mental Health[11] categorization of census tracts in terms of familism, residential life style, and community instability (based on seventy-five census variables) was available in 1975 and will be provided using 1980 census data. There are two other sources of maps and

---

9. Lakewood, Colorado, and San Bernardino and Oxnard in California, are said to have such centers. The one at Inglewood is financed by Community Development funds. William Ewald, a Washington Consultant, has developed more elaborate citizen data centers for other California cities funded by the National Science Foundation.

10. With the coming of the mid-decade census in 1985 this situation might change somewhat.

11. A Typological Approach to Doing Social Area Analysis, HEW, Alcohol, Drug Abuse and Mental Health Administration, HEW Publication No. (ADM) 76-262, Superintendent of Documents, U.S. Government Printing Office, Washington, D.C. 20402, 1975. These data were available from the State Mental Health Agencies.

information. The first of these are the Urban Atlases[12] issued for the sixty-five largest SMSAs (out of 262). For each of those SMSAs there are twelve maps illustrating various demographic factors.[13] There is also A Comparison Atlas of America's Great Cities.[14] For each city and its SMSA there are twenty-seven maps illustrating such data as population density, housing value, household size, and the percent of female heads of families. Following these there are maps and discussions on twenty-three comparative issues such as education, transportation, growth, segregation, and poverty.

There are also several computer services which put out tables and maps based primarily on census data. They are sometimes updated but the method used is often undisclosed.[15]

There is one data source which deserves separate treatment. The R.L. Polk Company publishes more than 1,400 city directories covering more than 7,000 North American communities. It has developed a data package[16] derived from its directory updating, which at a relatively low price supplies geographically disaggregated indicators of change to more than 300 city governments or planning agencies.[17] Polk data has received a fairly favorable

---

12. Urban Atlas, U.S. Bureau of the Census and Manpower Administration, 1974.

13. These included density; percent under eighteen years of age, over sixty-five years of age, black, over twenty-five who are high school graduates, labor force blue collar, housing owner occupied, of all occupied housing constructed during 1960-1970; as well as medians of family income, housing value, and contract rent.

14. John S. Adams, ed., University of Minnesota Press, Minneapolis, 1976.

15. The most prominent of these in the Washington, D.C., area are WESTAT, Dual Labs, and Applied Urbanetics.

16. User Guide to the Profiles of Change Urban Information Package, R.L. Polk and Co., 431 Howard St., Detroit, Michigan 48231, Feb. 1977.

17. During 1974 Polk data was made available to 318 "Entitlement Cities" through Community Development funds under the 1974 Housing Act.

analysis[18] and has been used in at least one indicator report.[19] However, in contacting cities known to use Polk data, there were more unfavorable than favorable reactions (four unfavorable and two favorable). Some claimed they had tested the Polk data against other methods of estimating population or housing and had found it too inaccurate. Also, in large cities the survey producing the data takes several years to be completed, thus the data is a composite of conditions over a number of years. Others claimed that interviewers went through neighborhoods when many families were not at home, that mail responses were accepted from those not at home, and that the interviewers were rude. Even though these data are cheap (twenty cents a household) or are available free from HUD, some checks should be made before using them. However, since the data often provide the only early identification of neighborhoods that are beginning to decline or improve, they should not be summarily rejected.

Two facts stood out in our survey of published intracity indicator reports. The first is that so few regular indicator reports are produced by anyone. The second is the wide variety of reports produced by city governments or planning boards and the difficulty in defining what is or isn't an "indicator report."[20]

There are many possible reasons for the lack of more indicator reports. Some jurisdictions collect such large amounts of socioeconomic data that they

---

18. D.W. Daicoff, *An Evaluation of the R.L. Polk Urban Information System Data: A Case Study of Topeka, Kansas*, Kansas Department of Labor, Nov. 1970.

19. Lorna Monti, *Social Indicators for Austin, Texas: A Cluster Analysis of Census Tracts*, Studies in Marketing, no. 22, The University of Texas at Austin, 1975, (see report no. 4). New Haven, Conn., and Providence, R.I., also use the Polk data.

20. Often indicator reports are called "socioeconomic data," "needs assessment," "profiles," or "state of the city."

cannot be published at a reasonable cost.[21] Also, officials who decide which reports to issue apparently prefer to address a particular problem on which some decision is being made, rather than to produce a descriptive document for the general public.[22] Reports based on citizen surveys tend to be expensive and hard to interpret, even though they do measure people's satisfactions with their environment and with available governmental services. Several research officials complained that their agency didn't have enough skilled talent to interpret such a survey. The problem, according to an academic respondent, is that the schools teach students to do only one-shot surveys and fail to teach longitudinal techniques.[23]

Thus, at the municipal level, work on indicators falls between the detailed data needs of the planner or policy maker and the simplification required in preparing a document that is both understandable to the informed citizen and of reasonable size. It also falls between the desire to have the public evaluate government programs through citizen surveys and the reluctance of any bureaucracy to acquiesce to such evaluation.

In the research and academic areas, indicators face a different set of constraints--on one hand, academic demands for rigor and, on the other, the need of local officials for workable and understandable descriptions,

---

21. For example, in San Diego they had two volumes of 300 pages each, and so they published only fifty sets at $50 apiece. In Los Angeles they had ten volumes of data. They published only 300 copies. (These two jurisdictions happen to also publish more abridged indicator reports; others do not.)

22. It is also claimed that it would be cheaper and more efficient for the planning agency to furnish, on a direct basis, the specific data needed by an interested citizen group rather than publish a larger volume of data for the entire city.

23. Another informant suggested that if the surveys were able to give the opinions of registered voters or could be broken down into different political jurisdictions, they would get more support and funding from the political community.

statistics, and guides to policy. Within the academic field, indicator work falls between the prestige and productiveness of academic specialization, and the difficulties of problem-oriented multidisciplinary research. Because of the complexity and multidisciplinary character of these problems, much indicator work lacks the theoretical basis which generally underlies work within a given discipline and shapes the direction of research. Thus, some may view the production of indicators as a statistical problem, while others feel that the function of indicator research is to describe sociological change. Others wish to isolate the economic factors affecting urban growth or decay. Also, few can be knowledgeable in each of the many subject areas such as health, housing, or criminal justice which are often included in indicator reports.

The academic world is not keyed to yearly reports (unless they are done by graduate students) since repeating the same report is not innovative or creative. Moreover, while publishing is highly valued in the academic world, the cities are generally more interested in using the data than in publishing them.[24]

We must not forget the problem of funding. At budget time an indicator report for the general public is likely to be cut in favor of a study that addresses a problem where a decision must be made. It is hard to institutionalize funding for the purpose of keeping the public more informed.[25]

Thus, the urban indicator field is quite fragmented. It has attained only limited academic respectability and is of low priority in most cities.

---

24. One city data manager maintained that she would rather reduce the misuse of data by discussing its application with each user than publish it and lose almost all control over it.

25. One of the jurisdictions that issue regular indicators can do so only because they are produced gratis by a professor and his graduate students at a nearby university.

As a result of many of the above factors the regular production of indicators has been institutionalized in only a very limited number of universities, research centers, planning agencies, or cities.

3. INTERCITY COMPARISON INDICATOR REPORTS

As shown in this section, we were able to locate only about half as many <u>inter</u>city indicator reports as we did <u>intra</u>city reports in section 2. When we examine them by type of organization (see exhibit 3) private research agencies lead the universities and both are followed by government (much of the research in the first two categories was probably funded by the government, but the exact amount could not be determined). The subject areas do not appear to differ significantly among the three organizational categories (exhibit 4).

The list of intercity reports indicates the variety of reports issued. As in the previous section, the subject areas, variables, and indicators are affected not only by those producing or using the report and the available data, but also by the beliefs they have about causality in the subject area being investigated.[1]

With respect to methodology, raw data can be used, especially where not too large a number of cities or indicators are being observed. The indicators can be converted into an index, or "Z" scores can be calculated. Sometimes weighted composites can be calculated. In other cases, factor or cluster analysis is used to group various measures that exhibit similar mathematical variations or characteristics.

Once the indicators have been generated, they must be displayed. The most popular form of display is tabular, although graphs and other figures are also used. Some reports use hand-drawn or computer-generated maps to show the spatial variations of certain variables or composites for various cities.

---

1. Since in many areas most people subscribe to the same belief system (and are often unaware of the possibility of an alternative), there is a great deal of commonality in the selection and treatment of many subjects.

Exhibit 3

ORGANIZATIONS ISSUING
INTERCITY REPORTS

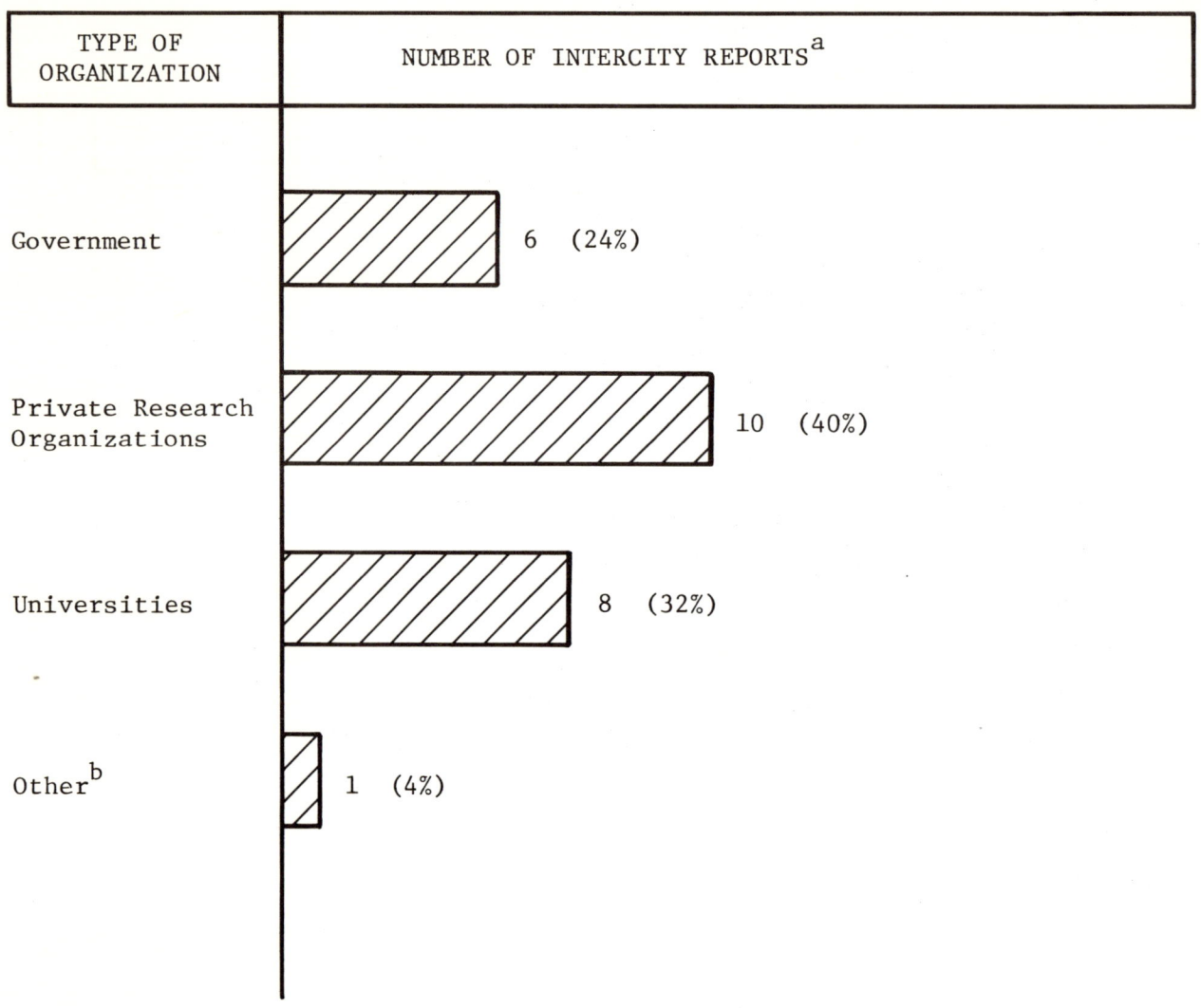

a. Out of a total of 25.
b. Represents an individual consultant.

Exhibit 4

SUBJECT AREAS BY
DIFFERENT CLASSES OF ORGANIZATIONS

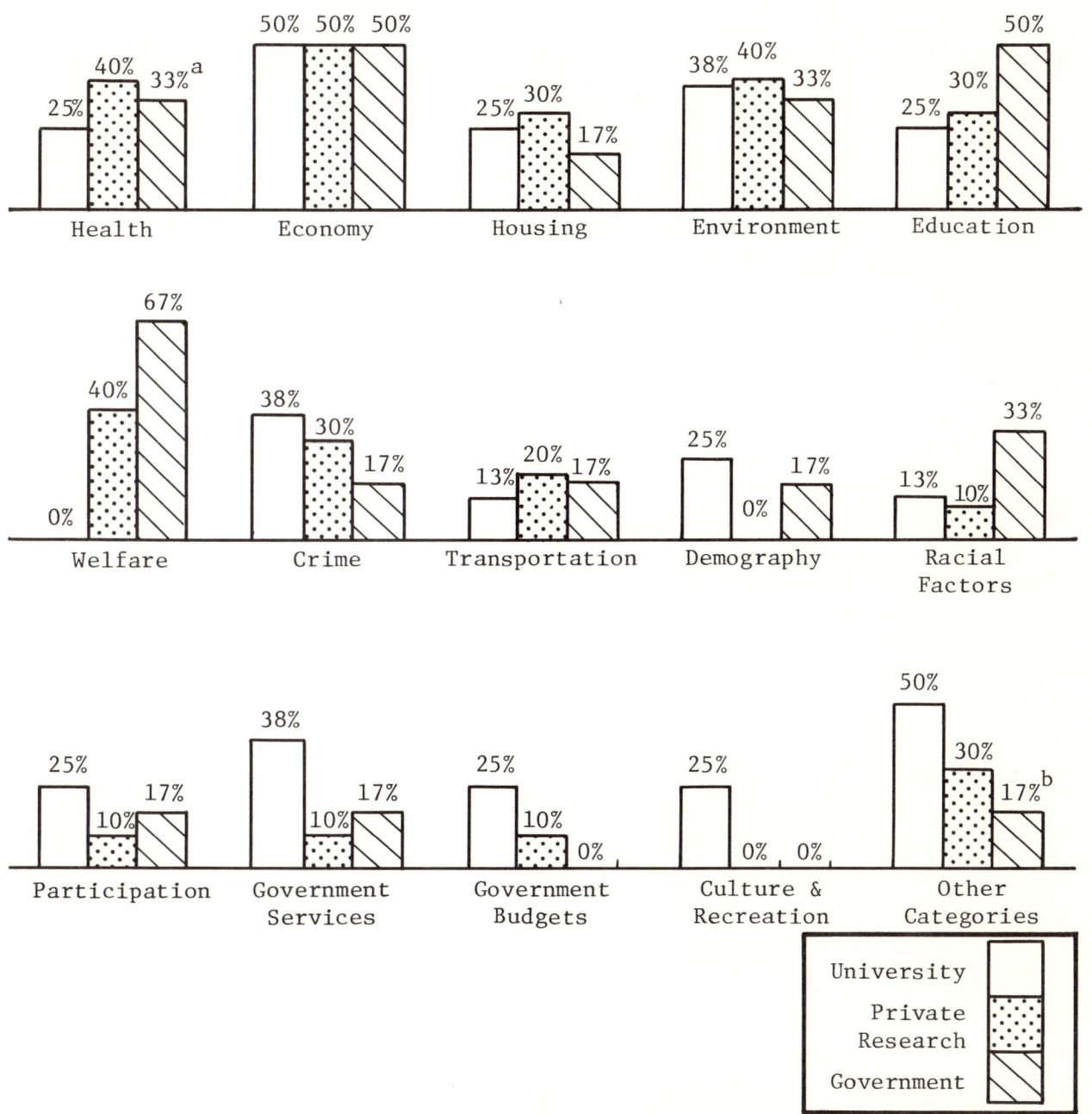

a. Of the 8 reports produced by universities, 25 percent dealt with the health area; of the 10 reports produced by private research, 40 percent included the area of health.

b. Of 7 reports produced by the government, 17 percent contained subject areas other than those categorized here.

These intercity reports seldom use data broken down geographically within cities. Some reports use many variables and make comparisons between many cities or metropolitan areas. Others deal with numerous measures confined to one functional area, such as crime.

Among the intercity indicator reports listed in this section, the one by Ralph Todd (no. 24) demonstrates a very compact form of comparing one hundred cities across eighty indicators. Each city is ranked for each indicator and a composite is calculated. Graphs of the means and extremes for each indicator are also presented. It would be simple to prepare a composite and a rating for any of the one hundred cities listed. To achieve this compact presentation, it was, however, necessary to ignore many of the limitations and inaccuracies of the data.

Liu (no. 17) also rates many SMSAs and presents a vast amount of data. His presentation and documentation are difficult to follow, however. Coughlin (no. 5) rates 101 SMSAs and uses factor analysis to categorize cities in terms of six dimensions.

The report by Sismondo (no. 23) is of interest in that he develops hypotheses on possible determinants of income and consumer activities and then attempts a test of these hypotheses.

Going in the other direction, Johnson (no. 16) presents a simplified four-page format which enables one to use the Statistical Abstract and other available data to compare his city with the national average as well as with neighboring cities. While this approach is crude it has the advantage of simplicity.

The Urban Coalition report (no. 20) presents background material, as well as indicators, on 30 cities.[2]

---

2. A Comparison Atlas of America's Great Cities, op. cit., would provide useful background information also.

Each of six COMP[3] reports (nos. 6-11) discusses a particular subject area and then uses data from approximately 30 cities to illustrate the discussion as well as rate the cities. The reports are clearly written and frequently use innovative measures and sources of data.

Regarding the data used for these intercity reports, one should note that there has been a great recent expansion in federally generated "small area" statistics[4] as a result of the need to allocate funds in general revenue sharing, criminal justice, education, manpower, and housing programs. Data on population, unemployment, and per capita income are now available from the Office of Revenue Sharing of the Treasury Department.[5] However, the accuracy of some of this data is being questioned. For example, the Bureau of Labor Statistics (BLS) has recently stopped publishing certain unemployment data for New York City, even though this data is being used in allocating federal funds. A commission has been appointed to do an 18-month study of New York City employment and unemployment data (N.Y. <u>Times</u>, Sept. 7, 1977, p. 51).

---

3. Council on Municipal Performance.

4. Mindlin, A., "Recent Developments in Federal Statistical Programs for Small Areas," <u>Statistical Reporter</u>, November 1972, pp. 37-48.

5. For example, <u>State and Local Data Elements: Entitlement Period 9</u>, Department of the Treasury, Office of Revenue Sharing, July 1977.

INTRACITY INDICATOR REPORTS

Origin of Report	Number of Cities	Subject Areas	Number of Variables or Tables	Analysis Used	Presentation	Comments
1. Advisory Commission on Intergovernmental Relations, Trends in Metropolitan America, Report M-108, Washington, D.C., Feb. 1977, 79 pp.	85 largest SMSAs	Pop. Growth and Density; Racial and Age Composition; Income; Jobs, Trade, and Taxes. (8)	21 tabs. disaggregated by city, suburbs, and region of the country.	Discussion of tables. Historical data from 1900 in many cases.	Tables	Informative presentation
2. Bullard and Stith, Community Conditions in Charlotte, 1970: A Study of Ten Cities Using Urban Indicators, with a supplement on Racial Disparity, The Charlotte Mecklenburg Community Relations Committee, Charlotte, N.C., 1974, 219 pp.	10 cities	Economic; Physical; Participation; Family; Housing; Education; Community Concern; Mental Health; Crime; Traffic Safety; Racial Disparities. (11)	11 vars. selected out of 51	Compared Charlotte levels and rates of change with average of ten comparably sized cities.	Graphs and tables (rankings)	Uses a different approach in evaluating racial disparities.
3. Christenson, James, North Carolina: Today and Tommorrow, vol. 4, North Central Counties, North Carolina Agricultural Extension Service, Raleigh, N.C., Nov. 1975, 29 pp.	6 counties	12 community services	45 vars.	Separate tables on respondent's satisfaction and on his desire for increased services.	Graphs and tables	Clearly documented citizen survey.
4. Community Indicators: Improving Community Management, The Community Indicators Policy Research Project, Lyndon B. Johnson School of Public Affairs, The Univ. of Texas, Austin, 1974, 135 pp.	6 cities	Demography; Economic Base; Education; Employment; Health; Housing; Land Use; Pollution; Income; Public Safety; Public Finance; Civic Participation; Transportation. (13)	71 vars.	Despite the large number of variables they all seem to be used without composites.	Innovative graphs and charts	Good discussion of the uses of and limitations of indicators.

INTRACITY INDICATOR REPORTS

Origin of Report	Number of Cities	Subject Areas	Number of Variables or Tables	Analysis Used	Presentation	Comments
5. Coughlin, Robert E., Goal Attainment Levels in 101 Metropolitan Areas, Paper no. 41, Regional Science Research Institute, Philadelphia, Penn., Dec. 1970, 107 pp.	101 SMSAs	16 Goals include economy, environment, government, and social. (16)	60 vars.	Uses factor analyses to characterize metropolitan areas in common terms.	Tables with standardized scores	Intercity study. Clearly documented.
6. Council on Municipal Performance (COMP), City Air, Municipal Performance Report 1:5, New York City, Jan. 1975, 35 pp. COMP is located at 84 Fifth Avenue, New York, New York.	44 cities	Various pollutants.	5 types of pollution	Narrative questionnaire sent to 44 cities.	Graphs, tables, rankings, and discussion	Much information on pollution levels and what cities are doing to combat them.
7. Council on Municipal Performance, City Budgets, Municipal Performance Report 1:4, New York City, Aug. 1974, 35 pp.	80 largest cities	Budget-making modes and possible reforms. (1)	25 ques. from their questionnaires to the 80 cities	Mostly discussion.	Text and tables	Interesting discussion; little data.
8. Council on Municipal Performance, City Crime, Municipal Performance Report 1:1, New York City, May-June 1973, 37 pp.	30 largest cities	Public safety. (1)	13 categories of crime; 8 possible causes	Partial regression analysis. A questionnaire was sent to the 30 cities.	Tables and rankings, supplementing the text	Good explanation of general causes of crime and specific cities' performance.

- 37 -

INTRACITY INDICATOR REPORTS

Origin of Report	Number of Cities	Subject Areas	Number of Variables or Tables	Analysis Used	Presentation	Comments
9. Council on Municipal Performance, City Housing, Municipal Performance Report 1:2, New York City, Nov. 1973, 35 pp.	30 largest cities	Housing. (1)	5 housing adequacy measures; 8 measures of city policy; 6 cost and income measures	Sent questionnaire. Discussion of demand and supply factors in housing.	Tables and rankings, supplementing the text	Good explanation tied to city data.
10. Council on Municipal Performance, City Transportation, Municipal Performance Report 1:6, New York City, April 1975, 53 pp.	28 largest cities	Public transportation performance and costs. (1)	6 economic and 7 service-related variables	Used multiple regression to predict public transportation use.	Text, tables, and graphs	Discussion of individual cities. More advocacy oriented than other COMP reports by the council.
11. Council on Municipal Performance, The Wealth of Cities, Municipal Performance Report 1:3, New York City, April 1974, 42 pp.	31 largest cities	Income; poverty; Inequality; Jobs; Economic Development; Strategies and Programs. (6)	26 measures of various economic aspects of cities	Numerous rankings for different economic areas. Narratives on different cities.	Tables and rankings, with text	Clearly written. Covers a wide range of economic factors.
12. Flax, Michael J., A Study in Comparative Urban Indicators: Conditions in 18 Large Metropolitan Areas, Urban Institute Paper 1206-4, Washington, D.C., 1972, 143 pp.	18 largest metropolitan areas	Unemployment; Poverty; Income; Housing; Health; Mental Health; Public Order; Racial Equality; Community Concern; Citizen Participation; Education; Transportation; Air Quality; Social Disintegration. (14)	14 vars.	Comparisons of levels and rates of change; also comparison of cities and their suburbs.	Tables, rankings and graphs	Thorough discussion of limitations of the data sources used.

INTRACITY INDICATOR REPORTS

Origin of Report	Number of Cities	Subject Areas	Number of Variables or Tables	Analysis Used	Presentation	Comments
13. Goldwater, L., Comparative Urban Indicators in the New York and Buffalo Areas, Division of Research and Statistics, New York State Department of Labor, Albany, N.Y., Aug. 1973, 23 pp. (based on the report named in the preceding entry).	2 cities	4 Economic areas, 3 Environmental, and 7 Social. (total of 14; based on report above)	14 vars.	Comparisons of levels and rates of change.	Tables	New York City and Buffalo data are extracted from the 18 area reports.
14. Harvey, Andrew; Procos, Dimitri; Elliot, David, Preliminary Progress Report: Dimensions of Metropolitan Activity Survey, Canadian Council on Regional Research and Metropolitan Area Planning Committee, March 1973, 37 pp.	2 cities	99 activities of people	99 vars.	Sample survey based in part on supplied diary forms	Tables	Shows different activity patterns by city and by other demographic breakdowns.
15. Hughes, J.W., Urban Indicators, Metropolitan Evaluation, and Public Policy, Center for Urban Policy Research, Rutgers University, New Brunswick, N.J., Feb. 1973, 231 pp.	190 SMSAs grouped by regions	Social area analysis: 1. Social Rank, 2. Urbanization, and 3. Segregation	24 vars. with highest loadings on the social area dimensions	Detailed exposition and test of social area analysis. Factor analysis regression	Text and tables	Clear exposition of a complex subject

INTRACITY INDICATOR REPORTS

Origin of Report	Number of Cities	Subject Areas	Number of Variables	Analysis Used	Presentation	Comments
16. Johnson, Willard, An Index of Life Quality: How Does Your Community Stand in Relation to Other Cities of Its Size in the USA?, San Diego, Dec. 1973, 15 pp.	1 city (compared with U.S.)	Economic; Social. (2)	20 vars.	Used Statistical Abstract and City and County Data Book to get U.S. average.	Tables. Uses San Diego as an example	Might be good introduction to the use of urban indicators.
17. Liu, Ben-Chieh, Quality of Life Indicators in U.S. Metropolitan Areas, 1970: A Comprehensive Assessment, Washington Environmental Research Center, U.S. Environmental Protection Agency, Washington, D.C., May 1975, 309 pp.	243 SMSAs	5 components: Economic; Political; Environmental; Health and Educational; Social. (5)	120 vars.	Used factor analysis to isolate 5 components made up of 120 variables.	Maps, graphs, standard scores, charts, tables, and rankings	Interesting review of the literature. Some arbitrary assignment of positive direction for some variables.
18. Malizia, E., and Melvin R., Urban Indicators: Measures of the Quality of Life of the Charlotte Metropolitan Area, Department of City and Regional Planning, University of North Carolina, Chapel Hill, N.C., Sept. 1971, 103 pp.	15 cities	Social Stratification; Productive System; Sociopolitical System; Viability of Government; Evidence of Structural Deviance. (5)	18 vars.	Ranks cities for each variable.	Tabular presentation of data	
19. Milbrath, Lester, Environmental Beliefs: A Tale of Two Counties, State University of New York at Buffalo, Jan. 1975, 162 pp.	2 counties	Environmental needs, perceptions, beliefs, and actions. (1)	50 vars.	Text with illustrative tables.	Tables	Thorough and informative.

INTRACITY INDICATOR REPORTS

Origin of Report	Number of Cities	Subject Areas	Number of Variables or Tables	Analysis Used	Presentation	Comments
20. National Urban Coalition, City Profiles: A Statistical Profile of Selected Cities, Washington, D.C., March 1977, 3 vols, totaling 458 pp.	20 cities	Population; City fiscal health; Changes in crime. (3)	10 vars.	Narrative on organization, income, and expenditures for each city.	Charts and text	Informative profile of cities. Stresses concerns of interest to the Urban Coalition.
21. Ontell, Robert, The Quality of Life in Eight American Cities: Selected Indicators of Urban Conditions and Trends, Urban Observatory Program, National League of Cities, March 1975, 251 pp.	8 cities	Income; Labor Force; Health; Education; Public Safety; Housing; Air Quality. (7)	46 vars.	Description and comparative data on 8 cities and the U.S.	Tables and graphs	Interesting discussion of indicators in general, as well as measures used.
22. Shin, Doh C., The Quality of Municipal Service: Concept Measures and Results, Center for the Study of Middlesized Cities, Sagamon State University, Springfield, Ill., 1975, 30 pp.	3 cities	Street Maintenance; Public Schools; Police Protection. (3)	6 vars.	Sample survey measured inequalities and adequacy of services.	Graphs comparing cities	Seems to have practical applications.
23. Sismondo, S., Applications of Structural Indicators for the Measurement of Development: Selected Findings for Rural Communities in Kent County, New Brunswick New Start, Inc., 1973, 243 pp.	12 rural communities	Income; Consumer Activities; Rehabilitation; Mental Health. (4)	39 vars.	Factor analysis in terms of "linkages and fluidity."	Text, tables, and charts	Tests hypotheses concerning determinants of income and consumer activities.

INTRACITY INDICATOR REPORTS

Origin of Report	Number of Cities	Subject Areas	Number of Variables or Tables	Analysis Used	Presentation	Comments
24. Todd, Ralph H., "A City Index: Measurement of a City's Attractiveness," Review of Applied Urban Research, Center for Applied Urban Research, University of Nebraska at Omaha, vol. 5, no. 7, July 1977, 19 pp.	100 cities	Economy; Demography; Environment; Crime; Recreation. (5)	80 vars.	Two different ranking techniques; also does correlations between key indicators and the composite scores.	Tables; graphs of means and extremes	Much information compressed into a small amount of space. Any of 100 cities can easily produce its own set of indicators. Does not warn of defects in data used.
25. Wing, George, Measuring Potential for the Quality of Life, Division of Business and Economics, Indiana University at South Bend, 1971, 203 pp.	16 SMSAs	Housing environment; Economy; Health; Housing; Education; Culture; Community Participation. (7)	23 vars.	Comparisons by ranking and index numbers.	Graphs and tables	Good discussion of each indicator.

- 42 -

4. FISCAL INDICATORS

Fiscal indicators[1] differ from those just discussed in that they are more closely related to underlying economic conditions and budgetary, administrative, and planning practices. Among the users of fiscal data are those considering investing in a city's bonds; state and federal officials monitoring a city's budgetary, management, planning, and borrowing practices; municipal officials evaluating conditions in their own cities; and, finally, the taxpayer concerned with the magnitude of his present and future tax burdens.

Recently there has been increased interest in developing fiscal indicators. As a result of the New York City and related fiscal crises, the buyers of municipal bonds such as commercial banks, insurance companies, and others, have begun to make independent evaluation of city fiscal conditions, rather than depend entirely upon the commercial rating services.

The two leading rating services gather similar categories of information (see exhibit 5) but use considerable judgment in rating the bonds of any city. (See exhibit 6 for definitions of the rating symbols and exhibit 7 for some sample ratings. Exhibits appear on pages 45-47.)[2]

City budgets and the forms they take are related to the process of evaluating fiscal soundness. As documented in Reigeluth,[3] there are disagreements about the extent to which city funds should be disaggregated, consolidated, or summarized in municipal financial statements. Also, while

---

1. This section is based largely on discussions and material supplied by Henry Mortimer of the Urban Institute's Fiscal Indicator Project.

2. Others who examine public securities are bond underwriters such as First Boston Corporation, First National Bank of Chicago, and Faulkner, Dawkins and Sullivant (FDS and First Boston not only underwrite bonds, but also sell their credit evaluation service to other buyers or sellers of municipal securities). From George A. Reigeluth, <u>Reporting Local Fiscal Conditions</u>, Working Paper, Urban Institute, forthcoming.

3. Reigeluth, ibid.

much city fiscal reporting deals primarily with current conditions, there are additional efforts to describe the longer-term trends.[4] Some of the difficult issues that are still being disputed in municipal accounting circles are being studied by the Fiscal Urban Indicator Project headed by George Peterson of The Urban Institute. These include accounting for the declining value of capital stock and the cost of replacement, accounting for the value of pension obligations, the total and overlapping debt of different jurisdictions, the use of summary or consolidated statements, and accounting for dependence on outside sources of aid.

---

4. For example, see Thomas Muller, <u>Growing and Declining Urban Areas: A Fiscal Comparison</u>, Urban Institute Paper 0001-02, Washington, D.C., March 1976. Also, for a clearly written overview of urban fiscal problems, see George Peterson's chapter on Finance in <u>The Urban Predicament</u>, William Gorham and Nathan Glazer, eds., The Urban Institute, Washington, D.C., 1976, pp. 35-115.

EXHIBIT 5

FACTORS USED IN RATING MUNICIPAL BONDS[a]

Standard and Poor's

1. Economic Factors
    - diversity of tax base and employment opportunities
    - employment stability
    - per capita estimated market values, value of homes, retail and wholesale volume
    - overall comparative economic performance

2. Debt Factors
    - security required by banks
    - per capita debt burden
    - estimated market values of the unit
    - rate of debt retirement
    - debt service requirement as a percent of revenues
    - debt trend
    - debt listing
    - projected borrowing over a five-year period.

3. Administrative Factors
    - form of local government
    - professionalism in management
    - tax rate limitations
    - debt limitations
    - tax collection experience
    - legal revenue projections
    - basis of property assessment
    - planning and capital budgeting utilization

4. Current Account Analysis
    - fiscal performance versus the balance sheet data

Moody's Investors Service

1. Debt Analysis
    - planning and use of debt
    - structure of debt
    - burden of debt
    - history of debt
    - prospective borrowing

2. Financial Analysis
    - current accounts
    - basis of revenue system
    - relation of debt services to total and mandated expenditures
    - budget analysis of trends of revenues and expenditures
    - financial administration; i.e., procedures in tax collection, enforcement, and planning
    - history of financial operations

3. Government
    - adequate professionalism, and diffusion of powers and responsibilities
    - adequate services for revenue base
    - intergovernmental support
    - competent administrators supported by managerial tools

4. Economic
    - natural resources of location
    - population characteristics
    - economic structure and trends
    - economic performance and prospects

---

a. This material was paraphrased from the following references: Standard and Poor's Municipal Bond Ratings, Rating Criteria, Standard and Poor's Corporation, New York, New York. Moody's Investors Service, Inc., Analytical Factors in Municipal Bond Ratings, Moody's Investors Service, Inc., New York, New York.

EXHIBIT 6

THE MEANING OF RATING SYMBOLS[a]

Standard and Poor's

AAA   Prime, highest quality

AA   High Grade. Second strongest capacity

A   Good Grade: safe but for possible weakness in one of the rating factors

BBB   Medium Grade: the lowest investment grade security rating. More than one weakness in the rating factors or one substantial weakness.

BB   Speculative Grade

B   Low Grade: investment characteristics are non-existent. Default could be imminent

D   Default: payment of interest or principal is in arrears

NCR   No Contract Rating. (No rating.)

Provisional Ratings: (the letter "p" follows the rating) Payment depends on timely completion of the project.

Moody's

Aaa   Best quality

Aa   High Quality, but with less margin than above

A   Upper Medium Grade: some elements suggesting impairment in the future

Baa   Medium Grade: protective elements lacking in the future. Have both investment and speculative characteristics.

Ba   Speculative Grade

B   No desirable investment characteristics.

Caa   May be in default

Ca   Highly speculative

C   Extremely poor prospects of ever attaining any investment standing

CON   Depends on completion of some act.

Bonds in the A or Baa groups which Moody's believes have the strongest investment attributes are designated by A 1 and Baa 1.

---

a. This material was paraphrased from the following references: Standard and Poor's Municipal Bond Ratings, Rating Criteria, Standard and Poor's Corporation, New York, New York. Moody's Investors Service, Inc., Analytical Factors in Municipal Bond Ratings, Moody's Investors Service, Inc., New York, New York.

EXHIBIT 7

MOODY'S RATINGS OF SOME LARGE CITIES[a]

Atlanta, Ga	Aa	Newark, N.J.	Baa
Baltimore, Md.	A	New Orleans, La.	A-1
Boston, Mass.	A	New York, N.Y.	A
Buffalo, N.Y.	A	Norfolk, Va.	Aa
Cincinnati, Ohio	Aa	Oklahoma City, Okla.	A
Cleveland, Ohio	A	Philadelphia, Pa.	Baa
Columbus, Ohio	Aa	Phoenix, Ariz.	Aa
Dallas, Tex.	Aaa	Portland, Maine	Aaa
Dayton, Ohio	Aa	Portland, Oreg.	Aaa
Detroit, Mich.	Baa	Providence, R.I.	Aa
Hartford, Conn.	Aaa	Richmond, Va.	Aa
Houston, Tex.	Aaa	Rochester, N.Y.	Aaa
Indianapolis, Ind.	Aaa	Salt Lake City, Utah	Aaa
Kansas City, Mo.	Aa	San Diego, Calif.	Aa
Los Angeles, Calif.	Aaa	Seattle, Wash.	Aa
Milwaukee, Wis.	Aaa	Wichita, Kans.	A-1
Minneapolis, Minn.	Aaa		

----

a. Council on Municipal Performance, <u>City Budgets</u>, Municipal Performance Report 1:4, August 1974, p. 31.

5. OTHER INTERCITY REPORTS

In this category we refer to reports in which the indicators are not primarily descriptive as in the intracity and intercity category of reports, but rather are used to advance some hypothesis, to illustrate certain situations, or to suggest certain actions. One example is a report by Richard Nathan[1] in which he calculates municipal hardship indicators based on city-suburban differences and uses these data to suggest changes in revenue sharing allocation formulas. Other examples deal with urban fiscal and economic trends,[2] social trends,[3] and differences between metropolitan areas.[4] Thus, there are numerous reports which integrate indicators into some conceptual framework. This is a large area of research where it is difficult to distinguish between "indicator" and other research efforts.

---

1. R.P. Nathan, and C. Adams, <u>Understanding Central City Hardship</u>, The Brookings Institution, 1976.

2. Thomas Muller, <u>Growing and Declining Urban Areas: A Fiscal Comparison</u>, Urban Institute Paper 0001-02, Washington, D.C., March 1976.

3. William Gorham, and Nathan Glazer, <u>The Urban Predicament</u>, The Urban Institute, Washington, D.C., 1976.

4. H.J. Bryce, <u>Identifying Socioeconomic Differences Between High and Low Income Metropolitan Areas</u>, Urban Institute Working Paper 1206-6, August 1972.

DISCUSSION

The major discovery made by this survey is that so few descriptive indicator reports are published on a regular basis.[1] There simply are not sufficient incentives for governments or the academic community to produce descriptive indicator reports on a regular basis. The primary concern of planners and government analysts is to generate program-specific information and studies of direct usefulness to public officials. The academic community, on the other hand, focuses primarily on research that is more esoteric than could be comprehended by the public at large. Nonetheless, a primary objective of the social indicator movement--the provision of broad descriptions of the quality of life to the widest possible audience--remains valid. In retrospect, it is evident that those who provided the funding for descriptive indicator development often selected institutions that were not motivated to provide regular indicator reports for the public. Furthermore, even if such institutions did attempt to provide such reports, the costs of reaching a wide segment of the public with published documents would be enormous.

Therefore, if there is in fact a public desire for this type of information that is not being satisfied some new channel is needed.

I suggest that some modified version of the two alternatives to published reports already discussed[2] may help to provide indicator information to those interested citizens who are not now receiving it:

1. Some mechanism for facilitating newspaper indicator coverage is needed. The <u>Washington Post</u> and the <u>New York Times</u> are able to establish

---

1. In the following we are focusing on descriptive indicators only. There is still a need for research on causal linkages which will permit development of more policy relevant indicators. Likewise, indicators that facilitate both citizen and performance evaluation of a city's services are needed.

2. Namely, newspaper surveys and articles, and management information centers.

working relationships with research organizations. Other newspapers might be helped by some sort of handbook to guide reporters to the proper data or to assistance from a research organization.³ There might also be seminars on this topic at newspaper conventions. Some sort of pullout section similar to the League of Women Voters Election Guides might be possible.

2. Some modification of a mobile management center might be possible. A portable arrangement of charts, graphs, and tapes could be set up at libraries or shopping centers. It might also be useful at public hearings where detailed information is needed.

In conclusion, the lack of published reports is not an anomaly to be repaired by infusions of new money. To attempt to reach the public with regular reports would be prohibitively expensive if many people actually attempted to obtain these reports. Some innovative new channels are needed if indicator data is to reach even a fraction of its potential audience.

---

3. This might be a document like Carol H. Weiss and Harry P. Hatry, *An Introduction to Sample Surveys for Government Managers*, Urban Institute, 1971. Also examples of stories presenting indicator data in the *Times* and *Post* might be included.